George's Perfect Pound Cake

Written by
George A. Baines

Illustrated by
Marvin Alonso

George's Perfect Pound Cake
Copyright © 2022 by George A. Baines

All rights reserved. No part of this book may be reproduced or transmitted in any form or by any means, electronic or mechanical, including photocopying, recording, or by any information storage and retrieval system, without permission in writing from the copyright owner.

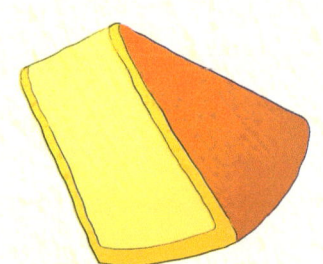
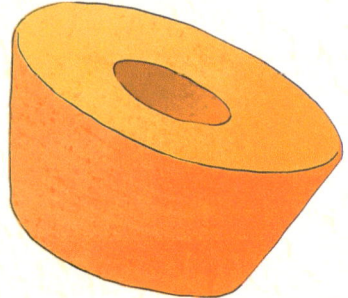

This book is dedicated to my mother and grandmother. To my family and to all those who remember those special times baking with their grandmothers, aunts and other loved ones.

George's excitement has been building all week
It's coming! It's coming!
He brushed his teeth. Check!
He washed his face. Check!
He said his prayers. Check!
Now, it's time to sleep!

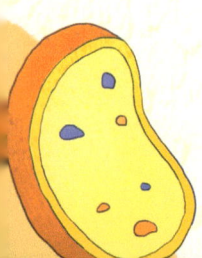

The next morning George sang..
It's Friday; the day I have been waiting for all week long.
I'm going to help Mom Mom make a perfect pound cake.
I must go to school George said.
While walking to the bus stop George imagined mixing the delicious pound cake batter in his head.

George could not stop doing cartwheels while waiting for the bus.
"Who likes moist....buttery....Pound cake?" He sang.

During school George couldn't stop thinking about all the delicious ingredients.

6 farm fresh, brown eggs, 1 pound of rich, creamy butter, 1 cup of refined sugar, 1 cup of unbleached flour, and a lot of love! Those are the ingredients which make a perfect pound cake.

After school, George and his brother Brian ran all the way home from the bus stop!

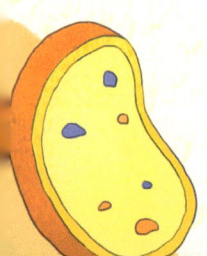

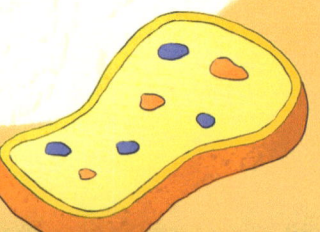

As soon as George got home, he greeted the nicest person in the world! "Hi Mom! I'm ready to go over to Mom Mom's house!"

"Hello Pork," Mom answered. "How was school today? Please change your clothes and eat your afternoon snack. Then, finish your homework and feed Peppy the dog."

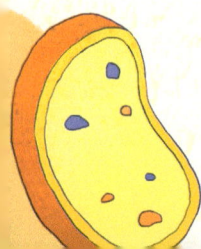

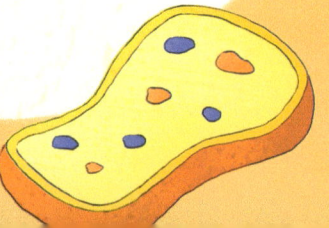

Later, when it was time to head to Mom Mom's house, Mom walked George across the street. She reminded him to look both ways for cars.

As he walked along the driveway daydreaming, George saw a bird's nest, he imagined the fresh aroma of the pound cake in the oven and the irresistible sight of the perfectly round pound cake on the cooling rack. Best of all, he thought about the big slice of pound cake he and his Mom Mom would share together.

"Hello George, "Mom Mom said.

She had the most beautiful eyes and the smoothest brown skin. George wondered if his Mom Mom would ever age! Next, Mom Mom, pointed her invisible magic wand at the kitchen table. "Let's check our ingredients before we get started!" she said.

This was a very special cake which had been passed down from George's great great grandmother to his great grandmother down to his grandmother and now to him!

George followed Mom Mom's mixing instructions. First, add 3 sticks of butter and 3 cups of sugar in a big bowl. Mix them together until they are creamy! Next, add six eggs straight from the farm. Don't forget to add Mom Mom's secret ingredients! Then, add the flour. MIX! MIX! MIX! MIX! AND MIX! Finally, George poured the batter into Mom Mom's special bunt pan. Mom Mom made sure the oven was just the right temperature at 350 degrees.

She also set the timer to bake the pound cake for an 1 hour and 30 minutes. Then, they had to WAIT....WAIT....WAIT....WAIT....AND WAIT! George knew, the only thing more important than making pound cake was spending time with his, Mom Mom.

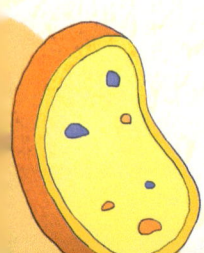

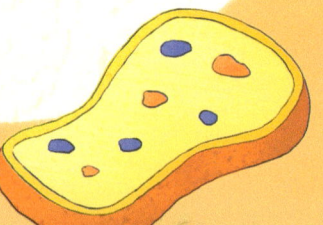

George licked the bowl while Mom Mom cleaned the kitchen.
Mom Mom, please can I lick the bowl, said George!
Yes, George you can! I am going to clean the kitchen.

Mom Mom, I licked the bowl clean said George!
Delicious! George cheered!

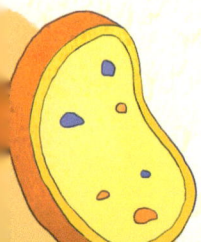

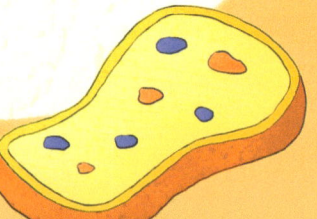

George and his Mom Mom has finished baking and placed the pound cake on the table.
I am going to save a slice for Mommy! I will also save a slice for my brothers and sisters, Joy, Brian, Missy, Ron, and Marie said George.

George gave his Mom Mom a BIG hug. Mom Mom, thank you so much for teaching me how to make your special pound cake. You have made my day. I'm going to call it *George's Perfect Pound Cake!* I love you, Mom Mom!

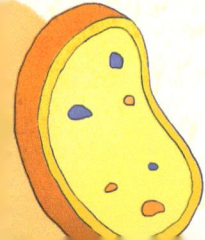

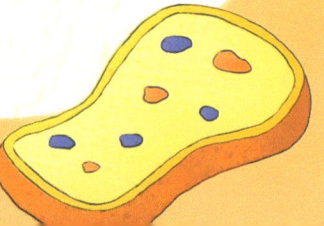

www.ingramcontent.com/pod-product-compliance
Lightning Source LLC
LaVergne TN
LVHW070434080526
838201LV00132B/267